GW01032844

Shepl

Patricia Cleveland-Peck

Illustrated by
Kate Aldous

One

"Ben, 'tis time!" A low whisper from his mother jerked Ben Tanner at once from a sweet sleep into the cold dark of early morning. "Are you awake?" she continued, setting the lamp down beside his bed.

Ben nodded, far too excited to remain drowsy on such an important morning. Quietly he slid from the bed he shared with his little brother, Tom, and shivering, put on the stiff new clothes he had laid ready the night before. A mixed feeling of happiness and dread filled him as he struggled, trembling with the buttons. Then, picking up the lamp and his heavy boots, he glanced round the tiny room. Tom had rolled into Ben's side of the bed and his young sisters lay like a heap of puppies in their bed by the window. The shadows flickered as Ben shut the door quietly on the sleeping children and crept down the stairs.

"Here he is." Ben's dad looked up from where he sat at the kitchen table. After a quick wash in the scullery sink, Ben joined him, and his mother served each of them with a big bowl of porridge.

"Get this inside of you, Ben," she said. "There'll be a proper breakfast for you, now you're a working man, surelye."

Ben smiled to himself. He had been surprised the previous week when his dad had told him to learn as much as he could at school as this was to be his last week. The under-shepherd had left the farm and Shepherd Coppard had agreed to take Ben on as his boy now that he was eleven years of age. To think that he would be bringing a wage into the family and that would mean more food for all of them!

"Eat up, Ben," said his mother, putting some cold pies into his new plaited lunch bag. "Your Da's waiting."

Ben's dad, who was a carter at the farm, smiled down on him and opened the door. The leafy lane outside was already full of birdsong as they set off, the man and the boy, for their day's work.

It was a May morning and the fresh sweetness of Spring was everywhere. As they entered the farmyard, swallows skimmed and wheeled, busy building their nests in the accustomed sites. Bidding Ben good-bye and good luck, his father turned into the stables to prepare the horses for their work and Ben, guided by the sound of sheep bells and gentle bleating, made his way to the sheep folds at the back of the farm, where Amos Coppard was waiting for him. Ben had known the old shepherd for as long as he could remember and a better man he could never have imagined working with. Ben only hoped that he would make the sort of shepherd boy Amos needed.

Amos told Ben that it was their job to take the flock, some three hundred Southdown ewes and their lambs, up to the Downs to graze there during the day and then to bring them back to their folds at night. He introduced Ben to the two

dogs who would help them with their work—
Tess, a shaggy bearded collie, and her son, Tig.
They looked keenly at Ben with dark, intelligent
eyes.

"Don't 'ee go spoiling them now," said Amos.
"Them's got to work just like you and me."
His eyes softened as he spoke though, and Ben
could see the dogs were very precious to him.

Amos then slung his big umbrella and his
lunch bag on his back and, taking his crook in his
hand, began to move the flock up the chalky
track to the downland above. The dogs kept the
sheep streaming up the narrow lane and Amos
strode smoothly along with Ben bobbing
excitedly in the wake.

When they reached the open rolling downland above, Ben felt as though he were on top of the world. He could see the River Midewinde glistening as it meandered through the patchwork of fields. Ben spotted his father leading a haycart out to the men mowing a meadow and thought how tiny he looked. Above, skylarks sang on the wing, so high in the clear blue air that it took Ben moments of gazing to locate them.

The sheep had spread out and were grazing peacefully. Amos told Ben to keep an eye on them while he went to see how far off the flock from the neighbouring farm were grazing. All went well at first, but gradually the sheep began to move down the hill towards the clover fields at the bottom. Ben did not know what to do. He ran towards them and a few scattered, then ran back up, but as soon as Ben started to climb up, they ran down again. Ben was becoming breathless and panicky when, suddenly, Tess bounded past him and brought the whole flock back to the top of the downland in a few seconds. When Amos returned and Ben told him what had happened, Amos began to explain some of the commands he gave the dogs: to stay, to fetch the sheep, to turn the sheep . . .

"But Tess knew what to do all on her own!" said Ben admiringly. "I didn't even have to tell her."

"'Course she knew," laughed Amos. "She's bin up here with these old mutton a sight longer than you, my young cocky."

Soon it was time to eat. Ben fetched his lunch bag, and he and Amos found a comfortable spot to eat their "bait".

Amos had a cold mutton chop and some "joe and harry", as he called his bread and cheese. He also drank some mild ale from a small wooden keg he carried. As he drank, he toasted Ben:

> "If I had store
> By sheep and fold
> I'd give 'ee gold,
> But since I'm poor
> By crook and bell
> I'll wish 'ee well."

Ben ate the cold meat pie his mother had given him and drank from the water bottle he had filled at the spring near his home on his way to work. After they had finished, Amos rose stiffly and said, "Now we'll take the sheep for their drink."

They set off across the Downs until, much to Ben's surprise, they came to a circular pool in the fold of the hills. It seemed such an unlikely place to find water that Ben asked Amos where it came from.

"Blessed if I know 'zactly," replied Amos, "but they do be called dew ponds and they never fails us."

This was just as well for the sheep hurried the last few yards and clustered round the pool in ranks; as one lot finished the next stepped forward to take their place, until all had drunk their fill. Then Amos whistled to the dogs, and Tess and Tig rushed into the water lapping and splashing; a few minutes' fun in their hard working lives. Amos allowed them a while and then, with a short note, he whistled them back on duty. They came out at once, shook themselves violently and came to his side to await orders.

That evening at supper, Ben had plenty to tell
his brothers and sisters. They were all very
impressed by his new status as a working man.
Later still, when Ben knelt by his bed, he thanked
God for giving him Amos to work with and the
sheep to look after.

11

Two

After several weeks, Ben grew used to the sheep
and life on the Downs. He loved the wide,
windswept feel of the place, the song of the birds
and the small flowers which grew in the short
grass. Little by little, he began to be able to tell
the sheep apart, a feat he thought impossible at
first. His favourite was an old ewe called Nanny,
who was very slow and had a job to keep up with
the flock. Ben would walk slowly beside her and
offer her titbits he had brought specially. She
learned quickly to take these from his hand.

Amos shook his head and said, ''She's trusting
like because she was a hob-lamb. I reared her up
meself when her old ma died.'' He looked closely
at her and added, ''But don't 'ee go getting too
fond of her. She won't last much longer.'' Ben
noticed, however, that Amos never hurried the
flock faster than Nanny could manage.

If Ben thought that a shepherd's life consisted of nothing but watching the flock, he was soon put right by Amos. There were many chores around the fold to be done. The hurdles from which the folds were built had to be taken down and moved from time to time, and pitching a hurdle was a hard job which Ben thought he would never master. Each day, too, Amos let Ben work with the dogs for a while and Ben learned a lot from this. He grew to realise that there was much more to being a good shepherd than he had dreamed.

One afternoon Amos told Ben to go home early. "I'll bring them old mutton down meself," he said. "You go on home and tell your ma you're to get a real good night's sleep because I wants you in that old yard an hour early tomorrow,"

"What for?" asked Ben.

"We're taking the sheep on a doddle tomorrow," replied Amos.

Ben looked mystified.

"We're taking the sheep on an outing," continued Amos, "up to the sheepwash, along past where you lives. And washing them is a fair day's work, you'll see."

The next morning Ben got to the farm early to find Amos ready, dressed in his best smock with a cowslip tucked into his hatband. Before setting off, he took all the bells off the ewes who normally wore them. They drove the flock out into the narrow lane which ran along the foot of the Downs, and Tess and Tig kept them moving smoothly, until they reached the spring near Ben's home. Today the quiet spot was utterly transformed. A field by the side of the spring had been set out with folds, and Amos drove his flock into one of these. Already there was such a hubbub of noise—shouting, swearing, laughing and bleating —that Ben felt quite confused. Farmers came from miles to use this sheep-wash as streams were scarce in the chalky downland area. Ben thought he would never know his own sheep again as the majority were the same Southdown breed. Amos just laughed at him, "This ain't nothing, cocky. Just wait 'til you goes to Lewes or Lindon Sheep Fair. *Then* you'll see a middling number of sheep!"

The stream had been dammed up to make a deep pool and two men stood in it, up to their waists in water. The sheep were driven into a fold beside the pool to wait their turn. When it came to Amos's sheep he counted them in two's:

> One-erum
>
> Two-erum
>
> Cock-erum
>
> Shu-erum
>
> Sith-erum

Sath-erum

Wineberry

Wagtail

Tarry-diddle

Den

"Den is the score, see," explained Amos, "and we pays for each twenty."

Ben wondered whether he'd ever be able to count the fast-moving sheep. He ceased his speculation, however, when he saw the men throw old Nanny into the water and push her right under with a big curved hook. One man then took hold of her and washed her heavy fleece, his big hands bright red with cold.

Nanny scrambled out a minute later bedraggled, the water running off her. She shook herself, scattering bright droplets in all directions.

"That don't hurt her," said Amos, noticing Ben's anxious face. "She's had many a wash in her long life and always felt the benefit of it."

Within a few minutes, sure enough, Nanny was grazing peacefully as though nothing had happened. Not so, the poor fellows who had been standing in the water. When the call for "bait" came, their legs were so stiff that they could hardly walk.

"Whatever they gets paid for washing," said Amos, "I reckons they earns it." He eyed his clean sheep with pleasure. "I always feels better meself somehow, when they get all that dirt and grit out of their fleeces. It justs blunts the shears and spoils the wool," he said, and added, "Come on, let's be getting our old mutton back to the farm."

Three

A few days after their trip to the sheep-wash,
Amos began to look anxiously at the weather.

"We'll need it dry for a spell," he said, gazing
up at the sky. "The gang'll be along to us next."

"What gang?" asked Ben.

"The shearing gang, of course, my cocky,"
replied Amos. "They're over at Eastease shearing
now and they allus comes to us next."

"Who are they, this gang?"

"Well, there's the Captain. You can tell him by
the two stars in his hat. Then there's the
Lieutenant who's got one star in his, and the rest
of the gang who are real hard-working men who
go round the farms non-stop until all the sheep
are done. They meets together before they starts,
at what they call the "White Ram Night", when
they decides what order they'll go round. Then,
when they've finished, they meets up again for
the "Black Ram Night" and shares out the money.

Quite a fair old drop of ale gets sossled that night, my cocky. I used to go shearing when I was first married and my Daisy would mind my sheep for me. Real work, that is, you'll see."

Amos looked at the sky. "I think I'll get some of them into the barn tonight, just in case it rains, because it ain't no good shearing wet wool."

The next morning the gang had arrived when Ben got to work.

"How'd you like to be our tar boy?" asked the Captain as soon as he saw Ben. The Captain was a big dark man called Musky Newell. He was already at work shearing, with shears like big pointed scissors.

"He'll pay you extra," whispered Amos.

"Yes please, Sir," replied Ben eagerly.

"Good lad," said the Captain without a pause in his clipping. "Our boy's got himself stung by a wasp. Got a lump on him like a bolster-pudding, so I've sent him home."

The next few hours were the busiest Ben had lived through. The barn and the area in front of it resounded with the bleating of sheep, the

clipping of the shears and the shouts of the shearers. A man would throw a sheep deftly onto its back and start on the fleece, clipping evenly until it came off as a whole.

From time to time the shout, "Tar boy!", would ring out as a shearer accidentally nicked a sheep. Ben would answer, "Coming , Sir" and would rush over with his jar of thick black Stockholm tar and put a dab on the wound to prevent flies and disease.

When the fleece was removed, the sheep, looking very naked, would scramble away as quickly as it could.

Daisy Coppard, Amos's wife, who had been a shepherd's daughter before she became a shepherd's missis, had come over to work as a winder. Ben had always loved her, for she was tiny and agile and didn't behave like an old person at all. Her laughter bubbled through the sound of the shearing all day. When winding, she folded each fleece sides to middle and then took a twist from the neck end to tie the whole into a neat parcel. She did this swiftly, throwing each fleece into the big woolsacks which would go off to the wool staplers at the end of shearing time.

In between, Ben fetched drinks of "swanky", or mild beer, for the thirsty shearers, who would pause briefly, wipe the sweat from their eyes and drink deeply. Ben also kept the floor swept, for Daisy grumbled loudly if the fleeces picked up any unnecessary dirt.

Towards the end of the day, the Captain asked Ben if he would like to have a try at clipping. One of the gang held the sheep and told Ben to begin at the back, the easiest part. Ben bent over the sheep and applied himself with concentration. He was getting on well until, suddenly, he realised that the sheep he was shearing was none other than Nanny. At once he became nervous,he might nick her. The Captain smiled and said Ben had a few years to go before they would make a colt out of him, but, meanwhile, he was "a fair ole tar boy and no mistake".

As evening approached, Amos told Ben to spread clean wheat straw up one end of the barn and Ben was surprised to learn that the shearers would sleep there.

"Ain't our tar boy going to doss along-a us?" asked one of the gang.

"Do you think I could?" Ben asked Amos. He felt excited at the thought of sleeping out in the barn on a straw bed.

"Best go and asks your Da," said Amos.

So, as soon as he heard the horses coming across the yard, Ben darted out to ask his father's permission. Luckily his dad had known Musky Newell from boyhood and agreed at once.

"I'll tell your Ma that they're a good lot, not a drunken crew like some gangs. No, you're a working man now. You stay with your mates."

There was little fear of the gang's being unduly riotous. They had all worked far too hard and by nightfall they were all weary. Nevertheless, they continued shearing by the light of a lantern until the Captain shouted to them to stop work.

Then they filled their mugs with ale, eased off their boots and began to sing some of the old Sussex songs. Little by little, each man found himself a comfortable place and, borrowing some of the fleeces for pillows, settled down to sleep.

For a while Ben remained awake, too excited to sleep. The sheep, penned for an early start, moved restlessly, as unaccustomed as Ben to their night's quarters. As the moon rose, Ben saw their yellow eyes reflected in the pale light. A barn owl flew noiselessly to her perch on the beam and viewed the unexpected crowd coldly. Ben yawned and stretched, the words of the song jumbling together in his mind until, at last, sleep overcame him.

Four

The farmyard felt flat and silent when the gang left later that day. The only thing that put a smile back on Ben's face for a moment was the sight of Tess and Tig, sheared like the sheep.

"I allus gets Musky to do them before he goes," said Amos. "They feel better for it, stands to reason, don't it, with summer coming on. Come on, now, my cocky," he added, taking Ben's arm. "We'll get the bells back on our old mutton and get them up to the Downs. We'll have to hope for warm weather o' nights for a while now, till their wool grows up a bit. You watch the poor things huddling together for a bit o' warmth."

Ben roamed about the Downs collecting wild strawberries and making garlands of harebells for his mother. Amos saw, however, that the excitement of the shearing had unsettled him, and that the daily round of bringing the sheep up to graze and then taking them down again at night had lost its novelty.

So, one day in the farmyard, Amos surprised

Ben by saying, "I've got sommat for you, my young cocky." He threw him a big soft bundle. Ben knew exactly what it was—a rolled fleece.

"This is off your old Nan, seeing you helped to shear her. My Daisy got it off the govnor for you, special." Ben was pleased but mystified. What exactly was it for?

"I am going to show you summat interesting," chuckled Amos. "Summat I hopes will stop you mooching about so bored-like."

He opened the fleece out on a clean patch of grass and, after picking off a few dirty pieces and throwing them away, he took several handfuls of fleece and put them in his bag. He told Ben to put the rest of the fleece away in a sack in the barn, which Ben did, still very puzzled.

Amos would not say another word until they settled the sheep up on the Downs. "Now, my cocky, just watch this," said Amos, taking from his bag a strange wooden implement. It was the shape and size of a tea-plate, but from the centre extended a smooth wooden stick about ten inches high with a notch cut near the top.

"This here," said Amos with a smile, "is a spindle." He tied a piece of thin string round the stick. "A lady taught me all this," he continued. "She was one of them walkers who come over the Downs from time to time." He paused and made a slip-knot in the string round the notch at the top of the spindle.

"A very educated lady she was. Bin all over the world she had, but she sat a-talking to me all day. She said all shepherds ought to know how to spin, like they does in the Bible lands. So the next day she comes back with this and teaches me how."

Ben watched as Amos took a handful of fleece out of his bag and pulled it and teased it this way and that to remove any dirt or seed and then, holding it against the string joined to the spindle, he lifted the spindle and spun it clockwise. When it finished spinning, he put it down flat on the ground immediately.

"Now, you see, my cocky, all that spin is trapped and to make the fleece into wool all we got to do is to let the spin run up the string, ever so smoothly, into the fleece, like this."

Amos pulled the piece of fleece out gently and Ben watched as the "spin" travelled up, converting it into strong fibre. As soon as that piece of fleece was used up, Amos teased another out and held it against the end of the spun piece and spun them together. They seemed to join very easily.

"Won't it come apart?" asked Ben.

"No. You feel. Real strong it is."

Ben tugged at the thick strand which was every bit as strong as the original piece of string. Amos continued until the length of wool he had spun became too long and he could no longer lift the spindle off the ground. He then untied the slip-knot and wound the wool round the base of the stick, making a fresh slip-knot round the notch with the spun wool.

"Now, you have a go," said Amos, handing Ben the spindle. Ben tried and, although the yarn did break once or twice, it was easy to rejoin and, bit by bit, he found himself converting Nanny's fleece into wool.

"The hours up here get lonesome for a young

'un, I know," said Amos, as he helped Ben with another length. "The old sheep and this around ...", he pointed to the open downland, "... is all I need at my time o'life and ..." he patted his smock pocket, "... 'course I got the Book." Ben had noticed that Amos carried a tattered old Bible which he took out to read from time to time.

"But *you* needs some sort of a pastime, and I think this spinning might be just the thing. When you've spun a middling bit, we'll wash it in rain water and dry it in the sun and then I'll show you how to knit it into a muffler or summat. I showed my Daisy years back and she's got real good at it. She's got one 'o them spinning wheels at home, makes all my small clothes, she do, and they keeps me real healthy."

Ben learned a great many things just listening to Amos. He knew all the birds, the skylarks which sang on the wing, the yellowhammers on the gorse and the wheatears which make their nests in rabbit burrows.

"Most shepherds catch them little birds," said Amos with a touch of sadness. "Eighteen pence a dozen some poultry shops pays for them. 'Shepherd's perks' they calls it, but I don't 'zactly know. What's eighteen pence compared with a dozen little birds flying free?"

Many wild flowers grew in the short sweet downland turf; burnet roses, scabious, vetches and wild orchids. Wild thyme made a scented and springy carpet and Ben loved to lie on it and watch the tiny insects and hodmandods, as Amos called the snails, going about their lives. He hated to disturb any of them and would lie quite still. The flowers attracted butterflies and Amos showed Ben how to hold a raisin near a butterfly so quietly that she would settle and drink from it.

As the summer grew hotter, Ben and Amos were often glad to use the big umbrella as a sunshade, and Ben appreciated the sea breeze blowing in from the Channel, which on a clear day could be seen glittering to the south of the Downs. If Ben turned his back on it, he could see the harvesters busy in the fields below, among them his father and the horses. When he and Amos returned the flock to the folds at night, they were often ragged about their easy life by the weary harvesters.

" 'Taint no easy life," said Amos bitterly. "Our harvest is a deal harder than theirs, and a deal colder. When they're snug in their beds come January–February time, then see if they'll want to change places with us."

Nevertheless, Ben was thrilled to learn that both he and Amos would be welcome at the big Harvest Supper to celebrate the harvest being brought safely home. It took place in the big barn which had been transformed for the occasion by Mrs Chadwick and her children and servants. Garlands of flowers and lanterns of bright colours, and a huge table laid down the centre with every sort of good food, gave the barn a fairy tale look which Ben could hardly take in.

He wore his Sunday suit and sat proudly between his father and Amos. Mr Chadwick, a kindly and well-liked employer, headed the board with his own family beside him. He rose and commanded the men to work as hard enjoying the supper as they had worked to bring such a bumper harvest home. As soon as everyone had eaten their fill, he and his family left the barn and the men re-filled their pots with ale and began to sing. This time Ben felt more familiar with the songs and joined in the choruses with a wonderful sense of belonging.

Five

A few days later Amos met Ben with exciting news.

"We're going to a fair, my cocky," he said, all smiles. "Mus Chadwick wants to sell some o' these lambs and buy two new rams, which will mean even better lambs come the spring."

All day Amos kept smiling. "Lindon Fair," he said. "It's an unaccountable good 'un, is Lindon. I'll be able to get a new coat and a couple more cannister bells for my ring. You'll see a middling number of sheep there, my old cocky, and we'll meet some other shepherds. First though, my cocky, we've got to get our lambs marked."

Ben folded the lambs, now as big as their mothers and distinguishable only in that, not having been shorn, they were much woollier. Amos prepared the marking iron. He showed Ben how a "C" would be branded into each ear.

"That way, everyone'll know that they are Mus Chadwick's and that they are good 'uns."

The branding took a long time, but Amos worked methodically until the last one was done. "Now we're all set," he said, straightening up with a sigh. He looked at the lambs with pride. "They're a tolerable good lot, and no one can say different."

The day of the fair Ben came to work early and found Amos waiting, dressed in his best smock with a bee orchid tucked into his hatband. They were to drive the lambs over the roads to Lindon some ten miles away and Mr Chadwick would travel by gig later in the day and meet them at the fair.

Tess and Tig kept the sheep moving smoothly along the road, heading them out of gateways with uncanny foresight. Ben found it no hardship to be out and about so early on a September morning, and he and Amos sang as they strode along. Ben had saved some of the extra money he had earned at shearing time and had it in his mind to buy himself a crook at the fair.

As Amos liked to be in time, they were among the first drovers to reach the village of Lindon, and Ben laughed to see the people run out and barricade their garden gates.

"Come tonight," said Amos with a wink and a smile, "they'll be running out again, surelye, with their brushes and pails to collect all them droppings for their gardens!"

Ben noticed that the villagers had been thoughtful enough to put covers over the open drains so that the sheep didn't catch their feet in them.

Soon they reached the big green, today covered with pens for the sheep. They soon found somewhere to fold their lambs. Amos went off to talk to old friends and Ben watched as more and more sheep arrived. Never had Ben seen so many sheep or heard such a symphony of bleating. As more and more droves came into the village, the narrow street became so tightly packed with sheep that, at one point, the dogs were running along the backs of the sheep trying to move them.

Ben saw that Mr Chadwick had arrived and that he and Amos were looking the rams over. They nodded and shook their heads and seemed to have decided which they liked best. First, however, came the lamb sales and Amos was very pleased with the price his pen reached. Ram prices, however, ran correspondingly high, and Ben gasped when he heard what Mr Chadwick had paid for the pedigree Southdown rams.

''Yes, they're worth a deal more 'n you and me put together, my cocky,'' said Amos thoughtfully. ''Tis a wonder Mus Chadwick trusts us to take them home for him. You think he'd sit them up in the gig and drive them home himself like the quality gentlemen they are.''

As lunchtime approached, a most delicious aroma spread round the green. A large fire had been lit and a vendor was roasting cuts of pork on a big round spit. Amos treated Ben to a piece, and they sat together eating the tasty meat with its crisp golden crackling between chunks of home-made bread.

Amos then bought his winter coat, a long white fleecy garment with a big caped yoke. Then he helped Ben to choose his first crook, testing dozens until they found one just right in height and weight and general feel.

"Your best friend, that can be, or your most tarble enemy, so you don't want to go choosing a latchety one."

After this, they wandered round looking at the shepherds' gear for sale. Lanterns ("We'll take one o' them—come in handy next lambing time"), coats, umbrellas, smocks (which Amos always called "round frocks"), billycock hats, shears and bells. Amos spent a long time listening to the different bells and ended up buying three—two cannister bells and a clucket, which he said would improve the notes in his "ring". Ben had begun to understand the old shepherd's love of his sheep bells and the way the chance ringing of the different notes, as the sheep moved about the Downs, created a strange music.

Laden and contented, they eventually made their way homewards. The two rams behaved perfectly, trotting delicately along in front of Tess and Tig. The only problem was Amos's new coat. The best method of transporting it had seemed to Amos to wear it, but he soon grew hot and red-faced. Ben felt sorry for him and offered to carry it for a while. Amos, who was tired, accused him of trailing it in the dirt. Ben, who was also tired, denied this. In the end they tied it up in a bundle and Amos put it on his back. They reached home without further argument, Amos, however, admitting that he felt "fair beezled".

The two new rams were introduced gradually to the old ones and, after a few glaring and head-banging confrontations, the order of superiority was worked out to mutual satisfaction and they settled down to live in peace together. The rams were then introduced to the ewes, where their reception was more friendly. They stayed with them for some weeks to ensure a good crop of lambs in the spring.

Six

Little by little the heat was going out of the year. Ben spent time gathering the last blackberries for his mother to make bramble jelly, a favourite with the family. He also searched for mushrooms on his way to work and, if he found any, he would wrap them in a giant leaf to take home at night so that his mother could fry them for his supper.

The colours began their subtle changes—the beech woods hanging on the sides of the Downs turning from green to gold, the stubble fields turning from gold to rich brown as the plough worked its autumn ribbing over them.

The days became shorter and colder, and fine weather became a bonus rather than something to be expected. Ben's mother cut up one of his father's old coats to make Ben something to wear. Amos started to wear his white fleecy coat and his umbrella now offered shelter from the rain rather than sun. With its help, even in the worst weather, when the seagulls flew straight past them into the more cosy wealden valleys, Ben and Amos could construct a shelter. By putting up the umbrella and backing into a gorse bush, they made a snug, if prickly, little tent. There, with the flock in sight, Amos told Ben of his long life shepherding and began to teach him how to knit the wool he had spun. Many a dropped stitch Amos picked up for Ben before he got the hang of it, but Ben became very keen on knitting when he realised that the answer to the problem of Christmas presents for his family was literally in his own hands.

As the goodness went out of the grass, the sheep were folded nearer the farm, first on the grattans or stubble fields, then on crops specially grown for them. The rest of the farm was busy with the ploughing, and Ben enjoyed seeing the great teams of oxen working in the fields.

One day Amos asked Ben if he would like to watch the ox-shoeing which was taking place in the yard. Ben was delighted and jumped up on the flint wall to get a good view. One by one— Lamb, Leader, Pilot, Pedlar, Quick, Nimble, Lightly and Lot—the big conker-coloured Sussex oxen were brought in. As oxen cannot learn to offer the foot to the farrier as horses do, each had to be thrown on the ground and the foot tied on a sort of tripod. The ox-man was a friend of Ben's father and, when he saw Ben sitting on the wall, he asked him to jump down and sit on the beast's head to keep him still. Ben did as he was bid, but not without a twinge of fear, especially when Lightly raised his head and let out a dreadful bellow. Ben realised from the wild look in the animal's blue-black eyes that he was terrified and

so he spoke gently to him, trying to soothe him
with words as he had heard Amos do with
frightened sheep. As each cue, or half shoe, was
nailed on, the nail was selected from a piece of fat
pork which served nicely as a pin-cushion while
at the same time supplying the nail with just the
right amount of grease. At the end of the shoeing
session, the piece of pork was given to Ben as a
reward and he accepted it gladly, knowing that
his mother would be able to make a tasty meal
from it.

Being a working man did not stop the excitement mounting in Ben as usual as Christmas approached. Mr Chadwick was a fair and kindly employer and everyone who worked for him had good roast meat for his Christmas dinner. Not only the food but the company of aunts and uncles and many cousins made Christmas the merriest time of year for Ben.

He was very surprised, however, to learn that Amos would not be going home for Christmas dinner, nor would Daisy expect him to. He would spend the day with the sheep as usual, his celebrations beginning only at tea-time.

Half-heartedly, Ben offered to work with him. Amos, with twinkling eyes, said "No, young cocky, you enjoys it while you can. You'll get enough working Christmasses when you takes over from me and that won't be long with me getting so darned old."

Ben awoke to a frosty, bright Christmas morning. Already the tiny cottage was filled with appetising smells. Ben fetched his bulky parcels from where he had hidden them and ran downstairs to give them to his family. Never had he felt so keenly the pleasure of giving. He received from his family a good knife, one of the most important items of a shepherd's gear, but the thrill he felt as it was given to him dimmed in comparison with the feelings he experienced when the choruses of surprise, delight and utter disbelief rang in his ears as he gave each of them their gifts.

A woollen muffler is a fine present by any standards, but a muffler spun, washed and knitted from the fleece of Ben's favourite sheep by Ben and Ben alone, well . . . His father handled the thick woolly scarf, feeling it with his big, work-worn hands and muttering, over and over, "Mercy 'pun me!" His mother asked him dozens of questions and was not satisfied until he promised to bring the spindle home and show her how to "work" it.

The rest of the day was bliss. Aunts, uncles and a bevvy of cousins crammed into the cottage, each shown Ben's work with enormous pride and each just as amazed at his skill. Then came the food. The table was piled high with good things for them all to enjoy. The frugality of the year was forgotten and, on this special day, everyone was expected to eat as much as was physically possible. After the dinner, a few hours were allowed for the adults to doze and the children to play outside before tea was served. There was a big Christmas cake and enough mince pies for everyone to eat one for each month and so, by tradition, ensure good luck for the coming year.

As the company parted and the good-byes rang through the darkening air, Ben shivered and thought of Amos, whose Christmas was just beginning.

Seven

The first few days of January brought some very hard work. Amos took Ben and a couple of lads borrowed from the farm up to cut furze. Great quantities of the thick gorse were needed to stuff between the hurdles to make draught-proof lambing pens. This "bush whacking" up on the Downs proved tiring and prickly work, and Ben was relieved when Amos declared that they had sufficient. It was then carted down to the lambing area, a small south-facing field where Amos had his shepherd's hut. The field was sheltered from the cruel winds which raked across the high Downs. It also caught every bit of sun which shone. There, Amos worked quietly and methodically pitching hurdles, fetching straw and furze and setting up hay cribs. All the while he handled the ewes very gently as he settled them in their new quarters, for they were all heavy in lamb.

"Soon time for our harvest, cocky, just you wait and see."

The cold intensified, making the ground steely hard. Ben developed shocking chilblains on his fingers and toes which Amos doctored with an evil-smelling and sticky ointment from his box in the hut. Ben forgot all his troubles as he helped Amos to prepare the hut. He enjoyed sweeping it out and lighting the stove, and he hoped, above all, that he would be allowed to stay there during lambing time.

One morning as Ben arrived at work, puffing billows of breath into the frosty air, Amos, who was taking a trug of chopped mangolds round to the ewes, greeted him with an excited look in his old blue eyes.

"You come and see," he said, ushering Ben into one of the straw-lined cubicles they had built, "the first new 'un of the season, born half-hour back."

Ben was entranced by the white fragility of the little lamb. The ewe was lying down peacefully, but struggled to her feet at their approach. She uttered a warning bleat and the lamb answered with his high "baaa". Then punching at its mother, put its head under her to feed, its tiny tail wagging vigorously.

Ben watched for a while longer and then went round the cribs with hay for the ewes. Amos returned to the hut for something to eat as he had only had time for a "dew-bit" before the lamb was born. As he fried himself some bacon to eat with his home-made bread, Ben brewed the tea.

"Look," whispered Amos, pointing with the heel of his knife, "Master Bobbie come for his rind." He threw the bacon rind to the robin which had come right into the entrance to the hut.

Ben begged Amos to let the him come and sleep in the hut and, after discussing the matter with Ben's father, Amos agreed. Ben made himself a mattress of sacks stuffed with straw and placed it on the floor next to the stove. Amos slept on a similar mattress on a shelf which ran across the back of the hut.

"You don't want to get too comfortable-like," said Amos, "because you've got to get up every few hours. Just keep your coat over your feet and get warm enough to get a bit o' shut-eye."

Mr Chadwick himself came to visit them in the hut and he brought a large basket of provisions which his wife had prepared. "My wife asked me to bring this for you, shepherds," he said, and Ben glowed with pleasure at being included in the greeting. "We appreciate what you do," he continued, looking round the hut. "It can't be very pleasant at your age, Shepherd Coppard."

"I've allus done it ," replied Amos. "Comes natural to me, Sir. I couldn't imagine the year beginning any different."

Mr Chadwick offered him some tobacco and they smoked a pipe together, looking out at the sheep in harmonious silence.

When he had gone, Ben and Amos unpacked the hamper and found game pie and fruit and cut cake and a box of sweets and biscuits so dainty and pretty that Ben didn't like to disturb them.

"You take them home for your brothers and sisters," said Amos. "Mus Chadwick meant that for you," he said. "He's a middling good governor and no mistake. You see he thinks a lot of his sheep, so it makes sense that he looks after us, surelye."

During the day, as they went from pen to pen, the snow began to fall. Three more lambs were born, including a pair of twins. The snow did not bother the ewes who were snug and warm in their deep straw nests, sheltered from the wind by the thick walls of furze.

Tess and Tig enjoyed the snow and scampered in it delightedly. When Ben and Amos climbed wearily into the hut for their tea, the dogs scorned its warmth and settled happily underneath in a straw-filled barrel.

"That way they keeps guard all night. That old fox, Master Reynolds, is very partial to a young lamb dinner and we works too darned hard for him to take one o' ourn."

When they were together in the hut, Amos would talk of the days long past, of winters so cold that when he came home at night his coat was frozen into a solid sheet of ice, of how he had taken sole charge of a flock of nine hundred ewes when he was only fifteen years of age.

"So you'll do, like as not, when I goes," he said. Ben hated to hear Amos talk of dying, but to the old man it was the most natural thing in the world. He laughed at Ben's miserable face and said gently, "I'll hang on 'til I got you tolerably well taught, don't 'ee fret, my old cocky. No, I'll manage a few more years yet. Come on, get that old-fashioned look off your face and let's go and see what our old mutton's produced for us while we're sat here jawing."

Two more had lambed and Amos knelt down and brought a third fine lamb into the world.

"Your old ewe won't be long," he said as they

passed the pen where Nanny was lying. Ben felt in his pocket for the titbit he kept for her, but she was not sufficiently interested to take it from his fingers. When they had completed their round, Ben went back to look at Nanny once again.

"Come quick, Amos, hurry!" he cried suddenly. Amos turned and rushed over to Ben.

"What you bawling for?" he asked, out of breath. "She's had a lamb, that's all. Get a hold o' the lantern and let me take a look."

"Is she all right?" asked Ben.

"I've told you a hunred times, she's an old ewe," said Amos, a fraction irritably, "an' a double is too much at her age."

Ben looked at Amos without understanding.

"She's going to have another," said Amos, getting ready to help Nanny's second lamb into the world. It was much smaller than the first one, but when Amos had shaken it and rubbed it, it breathed, then bleated and at last stood on its spindly legs.

"Come on," said Amos, "we'll leave her quiet for a bit. They're both healthy and she ain't doing too badly either."

Nanny, however, did not seem to want anything to do with the smaller lamb. Amos held it to her to make sure it sucked.

"If they don't feed when they're first born, don't matter how much they have from the bottle, they're never the same. They grows a bit, then dies on you sudden. So remember, they've got to get that first milk from their ma."

All the while Amos held it, the lamb sucked happily, but when he let go, Nanny pushed it away quite viciously.

"Why does she do that?" asked Ben, feeling sorry for the little lamb.

Amos said nothing, but returned the lamb to Nanny. Once again she tolerated its sucking while he held it, but butted it firmly away the minute he let go.

"Why doesn't she like it?" asked Ben again, his voice high with anxiety.

"I don't suppose we'll ever know 'zactly," said Amos, patiently putting the lamb back again. "They just does that sometimes, takes a dislike to one o' their twins. Don't seem to realise it's theirn own. Generally, what I does is take away the one they *do* like. More often than not, they prefers the other one to nothing. This time though . . ." Amos looked at Ben. ". . . This time I reckon your old 'un is trying to tell us summat. This will be her last lambing, so we'll leave her favourite and you can have the little 'un as a hob-lamb, bring her up yourself on the bottle. How'd that suit you?"

Ben grinned. He picked up the little thing and tucked it into his coat front as he had seen Amos do. He was determined that he would get the lamb to thrive if he possibly could.

Back at the hut, Amos showed him how to make up the milk, heating it to blood temperature in a pan on the stove and then pouring it into a bottle and binding on a teat from an elder stem. At first Ben couldn't persuade the lamb to suck and got the milk all down his trousers, but Amos showed him how to slip his fingers into the lamb's mouth and open it, and soon she was sucking noisily.

"She'll soon get the idea, my cocky. You feed her nice and regular and she'll make a ewe yet. Often the smallest born grows into the biggest in the flock," said Amos, taking the lamb off Ben and putting it into the compartment under his sleeping shelf. By the end of the day, she was joined by another rejected lamb whose mother had given birth to triplets.

Snow fell, muffling all sounds. Ben thought of Nanny, and when he and Amos retired to their straw beds, worry fought with tiredness in his mind. Fatigue won and Ben slept, but his sleep was restless and when Amos rose a few hours later, Ben struggled after him looking, as Amos put it, "fair beezled". There were several new lambs, including a sooty black one which Ben loved, although Amos was unimpressed. In the next pen, however, a lamb was born which, in spite of all Amos's efforts could not be made to breathe.

"Our first dead 'un," said Amos matter-of-factly. "Put him up there carefully, my cocky. We may need him yet." Ben put the tiny corpse up on the pile of straw without saying a word.

Later that night a ewe died giving birth to her lamb. Amos was much more cross this time. "A real shame, that's what it is," he said. "She were a good young ewe. Still, t'aint no use complaining, 'tis done now." He took her lamb, which had survived, and went over to the ewe which had lost her lamb earlier. She had been bleating plaintively and wandering round her pen as though searching for her lamb, so when she saw the one Amos held out to her, she sniffed it enquiringly.

"She's full of milk, you see," said Amos catching her with his crook and holding her still, "and this 'un is hungry."

The ewe looked puzzled and couldn't quite accept the orphan lamb as her own. Amos took out his knife and told Ben to fetch the dead lamb. He then proceeded to skin it, "easy as takin' off his shirt". He then fitted the skin over the back of the orphan lamb. At once the ewe looked more interested and allowed the lamb to take its first nuzzling sucks from her full udder.

"There," said Amos with satisfaction. The ewe began to lick the little lamb. "That'll save us a job, my cocky. If we get too many hobs to feed, we just don't get a minute ... "

Nanny's lamb, romantically named Moonshine by Ben, was, of course, his favourite but the number of lambs to feed in the box under Amos's bunk grew steadily, and each time they returned to the hut, a chorus of hungry bleats greeted them. It was a ceaseless task as they all needed feeding little but often, but Ben did not shirk it. Even when he began to feel seriously tired after some days, he still insisted that he should do all the lamb feeding on his own.

Amos was grateful. "That's a real service, you're doing," he said with feeling. "At my age, them bleating youngsters is the last straw! I don't mind getting up and going round the ewes, but coming back only to start on that lot . . . Well, all I can say is, I am more 'an middling glad to have you with me."

Ben glowed with pleasure.

"Yes," continued Amos, " I dunno how many lambings this'll make I've done. I know it in my bones. Come the back end of the year, I can feel myself getting ready for it." He stopped and did some calculating on his fingers. "Sixty-eight, I reckon, sixty-eight years of new lambs I seen. But seeing how it's all new to you, I reckon you're doing more 'an tolerably well. You'll make a shepherd right enough and a good 'un. You've got the right quiet way."

Ben blushed. He was more pleased with those few words than with any that had ever been said to him.

Eight

At the end of the first week, Amos did send Ben home on Saturday night so that he could get a good night's sleep and go to church on Sunday. Mr Chadwick was very strict about this and all his workers were expected to be seen in church, like it or no. Tired though he was (and for some reason he seemed even more so after a good night's rest in his own soft bed, than he was after his broken nights in the shepherd's hut), Ben struggled into his Sunday suit and set off with his family.

In church, he thought of Amos with the ewes. Mr Chadwick excused his absence—just as when a shepherd dies, and a hank of wool is placed in his coffin so that when he reaches heaven, St Peter will know his calling and excuse his Sunday absences from church, too. During the the sermon, Ben fell fast asleep and dreamed of ewes struggling in the deep snow. His mother wanted to wake him but his father would not, pointing towards the pews where the majority of the gentry were dozing as well.

Monday morning Ben was back at the folds, taking hay round to fill the cribs and mangolds to the ewes. For the first time, Nanny seemed interested in him and nudged the pocket where he kept his special bits for her. He spent a while scratching her boney head, noticing how thin she had become. He did not need Amos to tell him that she would not last another winter. He just hoped she would enjoy the spring and summer to come. Moonshine, however, continued to grow and was soon skipping and bleating and following Ben around making a nuisance of herself.

The weeks passed. As the snow melted, the jobs around the fold were made more difficult by slushy conditions. Amos complained that his boots were "all of a slub" with mud, but as the wet drained quickly through the chalk and the sun began to shine, this situation did not last long. All the first lambs were big enough to be moved to the adjoining paddock, and they crowded together to play "King o' the Castle" just like children. Moonshine and the other hob-lambs needed fewer and fewer bottles and began to grow large and woolly.

Then without anyone's quite realising it, lambing was over. Amos and Ben cleaned out the hut and locked it, ready for the next year. They moved the flock to the lower slopes of the Downs where they enjoyed more liberty. Tess and Tig were glad to be back in the old routine, and bounded about sniffing at rabbit holes.

There was a scent in the air which made Ben sing on his way to work. First catkins appeared and then shiny yellow celandine. All the muddy muffled winter weather began to give way to scent and song. Ben was pleased to see a yellow brimstone butterfly fluttering like a candle flame over a tightly curled fern.

Ben celebrated his twelfth birthday amid the flock of sheep which had become such a part of his life. Daisy gave him a pair of home-made carders, wire brushes which could prepare the fleece for spinning. Amos gave him a bell to put on Moonshine. At the same time, he showed Ben his own collection of cluckets, lattens and round bells, each with with their different notes.

Together they made some new wooden lockyers and yokes for attaching the bells to the sheep and gave all the old ones a coat of paint. All this was in preparation for moving the sheep up to the high Down, where it would be unthinkable for any self-respecting shepherd not to have the music of the bells ringing round him. These, and the cuckoo calling in the weald, marked the coming of spring.

So it was that Ben, a year after becoming a shepherd boy, was lying on the springy turf of the Downs, breathing in the thymey scent and thinking over the happenings of a whole year. Amos was standing, leaning on his crook, looking out over the flock, in his familiar position. From his teaching, Ben had learned so much, and he hoped one to make a shepherd worthy to take the

old man's place. He hoped that day would be far distant and that they would have many more years together with the flock on the Downs.

In the distance Amos whistled, a short high note. It was the signal for "bait" and Ben jumped to his feet eagerly. He and Amos unpacked their lunch bags in friendly silence and, before eating, Amos looked out over the weald and softly said:

The Lord is my shepherd,
I sharn't want for nothing.
He goes afor me over the green Downs
and guides me by the quiet waters
of the Midewinde.
He comforts my soul
and leads me along good paths
for his name's sake.
Yea, though I walk through shadowy ways,
I aren't afeared, for his crook'll guide I.
He'll find a quiet place for us to eat our food
after we've overcome our difficulties
and us'll be happy.
Surelye this loveliness
will be with me all the days
until I come to the house of my Lord
for ever.

Ben did not speak. There was no need. Amos
smiled at him and they began to eat.